Let Your Inner Alpha Loose!

• How to Be a Chick Magnet • Boost Your Confidence to the Roof • Develop a Charismatic Personality • And Dominate Your Life Like a True Alpha Male •

By James Beckett

Table of Contents

It's Time to Stop Being a Boy, and Start Being a Man

Why have you opened this book? What made the title jump out at you and make you want to dive straight in this very moment to turn its promise into reality? What's wrong with your current situation that makes you think becoming an alpha male is the solution?

My guess is that you don't feel like your life is quite where you think it should be and you're looking for the right way to turn things around. You think that maybe, just maybe, all it would take is a few tweaks of your personality to push you in the right direction, helping you get the girl, the high powered career of your dreams, the pack of friends you've always wanted to run with and the busy, rewarding lifestyle you know you deserve. You think that becoming an alpha male may be the answer to all your problems.

You're right – that's exactly what this book can do for you. But before it can start to do that, you're going to need to wake up to a couple of realities that are fundamentally, excruciatingly important.

Being an alpha male is not about pretending to be just like that one cocky asshole with the wry grin we all know, whose ego is too big to fit in the room. That's not an alpha male – that's an idiot with arrogance issues. You're going to need to understand exactly what an alpha male is before you can start reaping the benefits of being *that* kind of guy.

It's also not about putting on a front while staying exactly the same person behind the scenes. If you're going to turn things around and become the alpha male that men want to be and women want to be with, you need to accept that your life and personality are your responsibility and that changing who you are means deep, lasting improvements that are as true under the surface as they are above it.

You don't have the life you want right now, but it's time to stop crying into your cereal about it. You will have that life, just as long as you go into this process with the right attitude. Be honest with yourself and admit, maybe for the first time in your life if you've come this far as one of the plebs instead of one of the kings, that you can't be constantly making excuses for all the things that have happened to you so far. It's all down to you whether you succeed, and it always has been. Unless you accept that, you're not going to get far trying to improve things.

The only difference between right this moment and ten minutes ago, before you opened the first page of this book, is that you're now holding in your hands the secret to real transformation. It's still up to you whether you put it into practice and, like the butterfly out of the cocoon, emerge as the loud, proud and loveable alpha male you've always wanted to be.

Accepting these things is the first step to becoming an alpha male – congratulations, you've already started the journey. If you hold steady and keep committed, you'll also reach the end.

This is the last time you will ever leave the house not knowing how people are going to react to you. This is the last time you need to wait anxiously to find out whether you've got the promotion you wanted or you've made it onto the sports team. This is the last time you will avoid talking to the woman who caught your eye because you think she might turn you down. This is the beginning of the rest of your life – so let's get this show on the road.

What Does it Mean to Be an Alpha Male?

We all know what it means to be an alpha male, right? You see them all over the movies, on television shows and in books. The alpha male is the hero of every story and the icon we all of us aspire to.

The alpha male is the leader of the pack, the one everyone turns to when they need to know what to think or do, the extrovert who's constantly out on the town with his friends and attracts women like flies to the honey jar.

He doesn't take nonsense from anyone – and nor would anyone dare to give him any nonsense. He's excellent at whatever he decides to turn his hand to, from building things with his hands to playing sports and pushing his career to the next level.

An alpha male is charming, and everyone wants to spend time with him. He barely has time to sit down for a cup of coffee, because his calendar is so full of high powered work meetings, manly hobbies and nights out with women and wine. When he walks in the room, everything seems better and brighter – we're ok now, because the alpha is here to take charge. He's aggressive when he needs to be, especially when he's defending his pack, and he'll stick by your side through thick and thin.

In other words, an alpha male is everything you wish you could be, but you aren't. For now.

On the other hand, that's not all that being an alpha male is about. What I just described is a fantasy figure that the media has boiled the alpha male down to, a shorthand to describe a very complicated reality.

But the trouble with stories is that they never have room to paint the whole picture. They give you nuggets to chew on that help you access your own view of an alpha male, but they never show what's going on underneath. These stereotypes may help you visualize an alpha male, but they're not going to help you become one. To do that, you're going to need to go deeper.

So what's missing from the description? A whole lot. If you want to be an alpha male, you need to concentrate on more than just the movie version, and more than just the idea of being the dominant man in any room. You need to fix what's going on under the surface and, when you do, you'll find that it shines through and becomes visible to everyone around you, with no effort needed at all. To be an alpha male, you're going to have to become:

- Confident in yourself and calm in the face of criticism, knowing without doubt that you have fulfilled the promise of your character, but without ever displaying arrogance about that fact.

- Passionate about everything you do, clear about your goals and driven to reach the next step of the ladder on your journey towards success.

- Deeply committed to your morals and to earning the trust of everyone around you.

- Physically fit and healthy, able to take on any sport challenge or test of strength.

- Comfortable in the presence of others and genuinely interested in finding out more about them and helping them achieve their own goals.

- Quick to praise and feel happy for others' achievements, never feeling jealous of someone else's success.

- Tireless in your efforts to better yourself and your circumstances, no matter how difficult the path ahead may seem.

- Comfortable in the role of a leader and able to inspire others to follow without ever resorting to violence, bullying and intimidation.

- Humble in your own successes, allowing others to see you for who you are without feeling the need to flaunt the things you have achieved.

- Driven to succeed and to identify the flaws that are holding you back from doing so, never blaming fate or other people for your failures along the way and able to learn from your experiences.

These are the traits you need to aspire to – so did you find that list motivating, or did you find it daunting? If you're excited by the thought of embodying all those qualities, you're ready to walk the path of the alpha male.

If you thought the latter, even if you just thought it quietly at the back of your head, it's time to suck it up and realize that nobody ever got exactly what they wanted just by asking for it.

If you want to become an alpha male, you're going to need to work for it – and the good news is that you're quickly going to discover as you read on through these chapter that the process of working to become an alpha male, all by itself, is what's going to help you get exactly where you're trying to go. Are you ready to get started? Good, so let's begin.

Get Ready to Grow – and Don't Ever Stop Growing

You've already admitted that you picked this book up because you weren't 100 percent happy with how your life is going right at this moment and you're looking for a way to improve it. Because you already know things aren't quite right, it shouldn't be too hard to accept that you're going to need to grow and improve if you want to become an alpha male. If it is, then you probably don't have the mettle to get there, so think about your answer carefully.

You aren't an alpha male yet, and getting to that point is going to take a whole lot of personal growth. You're going to need to work on every aspect of yourself, from your attitude to your work ethic and self-confidence. But, above and beyond these things, the most important realization you will ever have as you strive to take your place as an alpha male is that there is no "end point" to work towards here – you need to embrace the fact that you're never going to reach the end of this particular leg of the journey. Once you become an alpha male, your job is not done.

Why? Because an alpha male is all about growing and improving, even if he's doing pretty good already. He has a laser focus on what he wants to achieve and he's going to take the quickest route to get there, which means improving himself and adapting on a constant basis.

This applies to every part of his life, from his relationships to his hobbies and career. There is no part of you that is perfect at this moment, and there probably never will be – but it's your job to keep improving every aspect of your character so that you are constantly reaching greater heights and achievements.

You're going to need to start thinking of yourself as a work in progress. You need to think in terms of consistent growth and improvement from this moment onwards, right up to the moment you take your last breath. You need to prime yourself to never again accept anything that's "good enough" and always be looking for better. You won't be done until the moment you're done – everything, absolutely everything, up until that moment is a learning experience.

It's a different mindset to the one that most people work with, and the mindset that you've no doubt been working with up until now, because most people see themselves as fully formed human beings who either fit the needs of the situation, or they don't. When they can't achieve something, they either give in to the throes of depression or find something or someone else to blame. That's why you'll hear so many excuses thrown around, such as:

- "It just wasn't in my comfort zone."
- "I could have done it if only I'd had the right tools."
- "It wasn't my fault, I just didn't have enough training."
- "I'm not clever/attractive/good at speaking/talented enough."
- "It was totally his fault, I should have been put in a better team."

What do all of these excuses have in common? Why, the fact that they're total nonsense. If you've used any of them yourself, or any that are like them, it's time for a reality check.

There are few situations in this world that cannot be changed and improved simply by looking at your own part of the equation. If you can't climb a wall, it's not the wall's fault. You can probably turn things around and get over the top of that wall if you work on your upper body strength for a while before you give it another go, it's as simple as that. If you can't find a job, there's no point blaming the managers who don't even know you exist – it's up to you to transform yourself into the right person for the role you're hoping to get.

An alpha male knows these things and embraces the simple idea that no challenge exists which cannot be overcome with a little personal improvement – or by otherwise finding a way to change the status quo.

When you fail at something, it's time to stop seeing it as the end of all things. Instead, you need to start seeing it as an opportunity to learn something new, grow as a person and find a new route to success. Didn't pass that test? Then you need to work out what you were lacking, be it time spent studying or dedication to the task, or something else entirely. Didn't get picked for the team? Then it's time to find out what your fellow sportsmen saw as your weak point and work hard on it until it's one of your strengths instead. Prove them wrong – that's what an alpha male would do.

What I'm trying to tell you here is that your alpha male self will never be perfect and never be exactly who he needs to be. And that's no bad thing. The point of being an alpha male is not to be a cartoon prince with a sparkle on his tooth and a kingdom at his beck and call. It's to be the kind of person who can accept his failures and weaknesses, identify what he needs to do to improve – and then go ahead and do just that.

Your school or college probably talked to you at some point back in the distant past about the idea of "life long education". They meant that you should keep reading books even when nobody's making you do it, but they were right in more ways than they realized. What they probably didn't tell you, though, is that learning doesn't come to you – you need to go out and find it.

The takeaway from this chapter is that you should never shy away from new things, nor decide you can't do something before you even try. If you're not ready for it yet, it's your job to make yourself ready. I can't do that for you, I can only keep on drumming it into your brain that it needs to be done. If you start to forget it, come back to this chapter and remind yourself of it – if you let yourself forget, you'll slip right back to the sad little version of yourself that you want so badly to get away from.

Normal men get stuck in a rut because they aren't prepared to put in the time, effort and mental strain that it takes to step up to the next level. Alpha males recognize that striving for even the seemingly impossible might be the only way for them to grow and improve. An alpha male then takes that challenge between their teeth and keeps at it until he's overcome.

Improvement Tips for Alpha Males:

- Write down a list of challenges that really scare you – everything from climbing a mountain to meeting new people. Jot down the excuse that you've always used to convince yourself it's outside your reach – and now figure out how you can change things so it actually is. Pick one thing from that list, then go out and tackle it – keep at it until you've overcome. And now you've done it once, keep doing it, writing new lists along the way. The challenges will never stop coming, and you should never stop trying to overcome.

- The next time you fail at something, analyze your gut reaction. Listen for the excuses you are making to yourself. Dismiss them completely and replace that train of thought with a new one: "This is just a stumbling block along the way, and my job here is to work out how to get over it." Push yourself to overcome the failure in the best way possible – by carrying on forwards, never backing down.

- Find your flaws. Which aspects of yourself are holding you back the most? Are you too lacking in conversation to network at an important work event, or too easily distracted to ever quite finish a task? You're not going to change things overnight, but recognizing where you need to improve is half the battle. It makes you aware of your flaws, which makes you more likely to strive to overcome them when they rear their heads and get in the way of your progress.

- **Make a change for the better.** It doesn't matter what it is – pick one aspect of your life, big or small, that you aren't all that happy with right now. Perhaps you're stuck in a dead end job or you can't bear to look at the view out of your badly located apartment any more. Work out what you want to change and then make a plan to change it. Stick to that plan, never wavering, until you've seen it through.

- **Set goals for yourself.** Alpha males never just sit back and let life come to them – they go out and get what they want. You have to make your own opportunities in life, and to do that you need to know what it actually is that you want. You can do this in every aspect of your life, from your relationships to your bank balance, career and aspirations. Don't set your sights too low, either – alpha males aim far higher than your average joe ever would, and they do so with full confidence

that they're going to be able to reach that high.
Once you have an overall goal, break it down
further so that you know what steps along the
journey you're going to need to take to achieve it.
Let's say you want to be elected mayor of your
town – who are you going to need to know, what
are you going to need to do and how are you going
to win votes? Keep breaking this down further
until you've got a task list to follow, and you know
exactly when and how to get each item done. Few
of us are born with laser focus, but an alpha male
isn't afraid to give himself direction and
organization to keep himself motivated along the
way.

- **Let go of what isn't important.** Take a look at your
weekly schedule right now. How much time are
you dedicating to the things that will help you
improve, and how much time are you spending
just playing around? Success isn't going to come to
you, so you're going to need to make time for it.
Unless you own a time machine (and if you did,
I'm pretty sure I'd know your name already), the
only way to do that is to cut out the things that
don't matter and aren't going to help you improve.
Instead of playing video games tonight, why not

work out, make a dinner date with a colleague or learn something new?

Get Confident – And Mean It

An alpha male is dripping with self confidence, it's what makes him so appealing to everyone around him. It's what's made you look around at all the alpha males you know and think wistfully to yourself, man, I wish I could be like that.

It's what's made all those women look right through you and make a beeline for *that* guy instead. It's why your boss passed you over for promotion and gave it to the alpha male in the next office. It's his secret weapon, and it's time to make it yours.

There's a subtle distinction here that you'll need to understand before you can move on. There's a difference between faking self confidence enough to fool the people around you and actually feeling content with who you are and what you have to offer to the world.

Faking it might fool the majority of people, but never enough to make them think of you as the alpha. They'll think you have an ego, sure, but they aren't going to feel that irresistible pull of a charming, self confident man.

So if you're not confident right now, you might be thinking you're screwed. You can't just change that fact, you're thinking, you're either confident or you're not. It's a personality trait, there's no changing it, and if you can't fake it then you also have no hope of making it.

Yeah, you're right, you aren't going to get far putting on a front, but there's still a solution. Your confidence is not something that's fixed, like your eye color or your height. It's partly in your genetics, but it's also got a lot to do with how you feel about yourself and the achievements you can boast of. The more you work on yourself, the better you feel, and the more self confident you'll become. And to be an alpha male, you're going to have to build your confidence from scratch and keep piling up those stones until it's sky high and everyone around you can see it.

How? By improving yourself so that you genuinely do feel proud of who and what you are. If you hate your beer gut, it's not about finding a snappy suit that happens to hide it – it's about changing your ways to get rid of the thing you hate and replace it with something that makes you feel good about yourself. If that means a trim figure, great. If you're going to need a six pack before you think of yourself as looking good, then that's what you'll need to work for.

Think you're probably capable of being pretty good at golf, or football, or cycling, but you don't really believe in yourself enough to try? It's not about ignoring your love for the sport and hoping everyone's fooled into believing that you don't really enjoy it after all. It's time to get over your fears and doubts – give it a go, keep at it and keep trying until you have a skill that you can feel proud to have achieved.

Hate your job and feel embarrassed when you tell people what you do for a living? It's not about phrasing your job title in a fancy way to fool people into thinking you're more important or more interesting than you really are. It's about asking yourself why. Is it because you haven't been promoted in a coon's age, or is it because you're in an industry that you don't feel people ought to respect? Whatever the reason, you can fix it, but it's going to take some hard grind. Dedicate yourself to finding the right career, impressing the right people or simply honing your talents to get yourself noticed. Whatever it takes, it's time to knuckle down and do it.

Are you starting to get the idea from these examples? Confidence is about feeling self satisfaction in every area of your life. It's about knowing you're working to the best of your ability at everything you're interested in doing and achieving. It's about knowing, deep down, that you haven't been lazy, unmotivated or scared – and it's about knowing that you've pushed past those emotions and achieved what you wanted to regardless.

This goes hand in hand with the idea of being relentless about self improvement. It's not something you can do half heartedly, you're going to need to put in all the effort you can, at all times. You have to really want this to make it happen, because you'll never keep up the kind of motivation that's necessary to reach those peak levels if you don't.

So ask yourself right now: how much do you want this? And if you aren't shouting at the page that I should just shut up and tell you how to get it done, you might want to take a look at your priorities and come back to this book when you're ready to become a real man.

When you declare that you want something like this badly, don't forget that you're also saying you want to fight the battle that's ahead of you before you can win it. You're saying that the struggle doesn't faze you and the stumbling blocks along the way don't frighten you, because you're going to get there no matter what. You're saying that you'll do anything it takes to achieve your goals – just like an alpha male would do.

It's a self fulfilling prophecy that feeds itself as you go: the more you work to improve yourself, the better and more confident you will feel and the more you will want to keep improving yourself.

Improvement Tips for Alpha Males:

- Give everything your best. Whether you've been handed a project at work or you're thinking of giving a new hobby a go, it's time to tackle it like an alpha male. Too many people hide behind the idea that, if they aren't giving it their all, they have an excuse when they don't succeed. They could have done better if they'd spent more time at the gym, or they didn't have enough time to research the paper as much as they wanted to. Alpha males don't think like that – they go full pelt into a project and, if it doesn't work out, all they want to know is how to make it work the next time round.

- Wake up and set yourself goals. A huge part of improving your confidence is showing yourself that you really can meet the goals you've chosen to set yourself. You'd be shocked how much of your confidence gets leeched when you don't finish out your list of tasks for the day. You probably don't even know it's happening, especially if you haven't really pinned down what it was you wanted to achieve in the first place. Your first step is to define those goals for yourself more clearly. By tonight, what do you want and need to have got done? Be specific. Be reasonable, but push yourself every day just a little bit further.

- **Think about how you can make an impact.**
  Another massively important part of self
  confidence is the idea of contributing something to
  this world. It might be that you want to be the best
  at something, you could be the kind of person who
  feels fulfilled by getting involved in their
  community or helps out with a charity. To become
  an alpha male, you need to feel like you're making
  a difference. It's up to you what that difference is
  and how you're going to go about making it, but
  it's not optional – you need to get started on it right
  now.

Find the Meaning in YOUR Life

We touched on this just a little bit in the last chapter, but let's take it one step further. Alpha males don't wander this planet waiting patiently for opportunity to come to them. They make opportunity WANT to knock, and they seem to get all the biggest breaks as a result.

I'll bet you've felt a few waves of jealousy in the past, watching as the alpha males get all the best jobs, the prettiest women and the most money. If you've ever sat bitterly staring on as a friend went on the vacation of a lifetime with his gorgeous, doting wife, or you've quietly hated him as he left on an all expenses paid trip abroad on behalf of the company who values every last noise he makes and every darned breath he takes, you know exactly what I mean.

But sitting where you're sitting, hating others for their accomplishments and muttering about how they can't possibly deserve it more than you do, is exactly why you're not the alpha male in your group. It's happening because, unlike that guy, you haven't decided what you want and you haven't made up your mind to go out and get it.

So what is it that you want from your life? Where do you want to be 12 months from now? How about in five years?

What about ten? And what about that very last moment when you breathe your last breath and shuffle off this mortal coil – where do you want to be that day and what do you want to have achieved? What do you want to flash through your mind as you climb the brightly lit corridor to your afterlife?

To figure that out, you'll need to do some deep thinking. Maybe you have a vague idea already, I wouldn't know, but you sure don't have a cut and dried plan that you've been following since you were out of short trousers. How do I know? Because you're not an alpha male yet.

So let's take some time out here while you ask yourself a few questions – and don't come back until you have. I want to see these answers scrawled all over a whiteboard, stuck with superglue to your fridge or typed up, printed and laminated. I want them solid and determined and fully ready for you to go out and start achieving them. I want you to answer these questions first, then fill in the blanks that come after them.

- What means the most to you in this world?
- What would you like to be remembered for?
- Who is it that you want to remember you?
- What do you want to have given back to the world?
- What do you want from your career?

- What hobbies, pursuits and talents do you want to excel at?
- What do you want from your love life?
- What about your family life?

With these things in mind, I want you to write down your goal or goals for your career, interests, achievements, love life and family in the long term. I then want you to break that down and set yourself goals for six months' time, a year from now, five years into the future and a decade on.

I want you to put it somewhere you're going to see it every single day, at least once, to remind yourself what the meaning of your life is and what you want from it. And when you do look at that list of goals, I want you to think about what you've done recently to work towards them and ask yourself if you've really done enough.

Have you just left them there, hoping they'll magically make themselves come true, like you used to do as a kid with a candle on a birthday cake? Or are you pushing yourself every single day towards them? Only when you can answer yes to that second question and chuckle to yourself at the idea of the first question have you taken this step towards becoming an alpha male.

As you get into this mindset, you'll find that the rest follows naturally. When you decide on a goal, you'll find yourself automatically considering how you're going to need to get there and thinking about the journey, rather than the goal. You'll start planning out the steps, asking yourself what you have now and what you need to have in order to grab that goal between your hands.

And you will have to do that because, as you keep growing, you'll keep unlocking more opportunities and it's possible that you'll find yourself going in an entirely different direction. That's not a problem – in fact, it's good. An alpha male knows how to spot opportunities and then adapt his plans to make the most of them. Whatever it is that you've just laminated onto a whiteboard and stuck on your fridge with superglue is just a starting point – it's the view from where you are right now, and things could look completely different from further up towards the top of your personal mountain.

What I want you to take away from this chapter is that there's a huge difference between you right now and the alpha male you want to be, and it's all about thinking of the future. If you're happy sitting around waiting for good things to come to you, that's just fine – but you'll need to put this book down and walk away, because it's not how an alpha male thinks.

But if you want your life to be full of meaning, constantly looking forward towards the things that you know you'll one day wonder how you ever lived without, then you need to decide right here, and right now, what those things are. If they change along the way, that's a good thing, just as long as you continue to push towards the real meaning of your life.

Never, Ever Give Up

What I told you in the previous chapter no doubt sounds exhausting. I've essentially just told you that there'll be no more sitting on the sofa playing Call of Duty until the wee hours and you'll want to think twice about switching on the television or wasting time browsing new gadgets at the mall.

I've told you that your life from this moment onwards is going to be a struggle and that you might not get to see the rewards for a good long while. Right?

Actually, no. I'm not telling you that at all. What I'm saying is that you need to reconsider the balance of your life and put a lot more effort into the things that really matter to you. If you want to be a gaming pro, go for it, and you can stay up all night practicing your virtual sniping skills to do it if that's what it takes – I'll be right behind you, buddy, cheering you along the way.

But if gaming is just something you do to kill time before bed, or you pick up the controller because you can't think of anything else to do with the gap between now and when you head out to meet your friends for a drink, then you need to ask yourself if it's really worth doing.

It's also worth pausing for a second to stress that, just because I had you write goals you want to have achieved a decade down the line, it doesn't mean you're not going to get anything for all that hard work between then and now. You're not going to be old and grey before you start seeing the fruits of your efforts – you might even see some of those rewards by the end of today.

Let's say you've decided you want to be a world class chef. Tonight, you decide to cook a new pasta entree that you've never tried before because it seemed too hard or like it was going to take way too much time to be worth it, or you couldn't be bothered to go out and hunt down the fancy ingredients. Because you've decided that you want to take your rightful place as an alpha male, the type of guy who wouldn't let any of that bunkum stop him, you bite the bullet and cook it. Your spaghetti comes out good, and your mom and your dad and your aunt and your girlfriend and your dog all tell you that it was delicious.

Bingo, you've achieved something, and you're already feeling good about the journey. The little jolt of pleasure that came from taking a step along the way is just your first taste. Most of the time, assuming you really do keep pushing yourself, you're going to be feeling little bursts of happy just like that one, pretty much every single day. Every time you look at your goals and know you've worked towards them, and for every tiny achievement that makes up the overall goal, you'll get a little tingle in your tippy toes.

No, you haven't reached the overall goal you set yourself, but you know you moved another inch towards it. And because that goal has sincere meaning to you and represents the true meaning of your life, moving towards it is going to mean a whole lot to you.

On the other hand, there are going to be days when you want to pack all of this in and go back to the time when you could go fishing all day and not care if you came home with a catch of the day for your dinner, or when you could just sit back with a bowl of nachos to watch the game. You'll start to miss your pre-alpha self, because he had it so easy. He didn't have to push himself, he didn't have to be mindful of how he spent his time, he didn't have to think about what every action was doing for his future.

You'll fail at something – of course you will, we all do at one time or another. You'll try to cook a soufflé to impress your friends and it'll come out looking like a yak threw up all over your oven dish. And you'll think to yourself, why the hell am I doing this to myself?

Or you'll hit a wall in your progress – some seemingly insurmountable obstacle that it's going to take a lot of effort to get past. You're tired, you've got things you'd rather be doing, you're busy or you're just plain fed up.

And that, right there, is the golden moment: the one where you test your mettle. Are you really just still the old version of yourself who didn't know the meaning of his life and didn't care? Or have you transformed into the alpha male who takes even failure as an opportunity to excel?

In that moment, you'll have two choices. You can either give up and toss this book in the fireplace, or you can pick yourself up, dust off the soufflé crumbs and work out what went wrong, ready and willing to use that information the next time you pull out your whisk and apron.

So if you really do want to be an alpha male, prepare yourself for the long haul. You're going to need to push yourself every day, no matter whether you fail or whether things get too hard. And you're never, ever going to be allowed to give up.

- **Expect the bad days.** I'll tell you right now why we have such a hard time dealing with failure and unexpected obstacles. It's because, deep down, we honestly think we can avoid them. We think we're special and that, because we've put in a bit of effort, we've done enough to stave off any big issues. That's a bad way of looking at it, because it makes the days when you don't meet your goals seem so much worse. You need to accept that you won't succeed every single time, that the world won't always cooperate with your plans, and that it doesn't really matter if that happens. You're an alpha male – you're fully confident of taking it in your stride and trying again.

- **Let go of the little things.** When we sweat the small stuff, it suddenly becomes far more important than it ought to be. It doesn't matter if it rained on your brand new suit, that guy who shoved you on the subway has no real consequence and you're not going to keel over dead because you trod in dog mess. Stop worrying so much about the little things in life – save your energy for the goals that will change your future.

- **Set up your own motivation system.** What motivates you will be different from what motivates me – hell, you can promise me a slice of pizza and I'll climb Everest by the end of the day if you want me to. You need to work out how to get yourself back on the horse when you fall off, and by that I mean you need to set up a tangible system that works for you. You'll see plenty of advice for that – stick up a picture of your flabby stomach on the fridge to confront you if you try to sneak a snack, daydream about your perfect home in the suburbs, stick your goals to a whiteboard with superglue and then laminate the fridge. You name it, someone somewhere has suggested it as hard and fast advice. So while you really do need to have your goals set out in stone for yourself, the motivation you use to get there will be personal. What will make you want to carry on when you've hit a roadblock? Work that out now, while you're sailing along nicely, and you'll have it ready to roll out when you hit bumpy waters.

- **Ignore the naysayers.** We all know people who think the worst of every situation and are prone to telling us we haven't got what it takes to reach our goals. I don't care whether it's your third grade teacher or your beloved grandmother, it's time to start ignoring what they say. Stop putting stock in what other people think and start having confidence in your own opinion. If you think you can do this, you can. When they tell you that you can't, flash them a shining grin, thank them politely for their input and then get the hell out of there so you can discard every last memory of whatever nonsense they spouted.

Start Thinking for Yourself

Are you pursuing a career because someone, at some point, told you it was a good idea? Did you take up football because daddy wanted you to follow in his footsteps? Do you go to the cool bar in town because everyone else likes it, even though you think it smells funny and you can never get a seat? Do you eat your meals at breakfast, lunch and dinner because those are the expected times for refueling?

Why? Why have you chosen to follow the crowd, even when you don't agree with what it thinks? Why are you letting other people dictate everything from the clothes you wear to the life you lead? Is it because that's really what you want, or is it because you don't know how to do things any differently?

This connects strongly to your goals and your self confidence, so I want you to read this chapter with a mind towards working on your self respect. I even want you to have an open mind about possibly changing those goals you set for yourself a couple of chapters back, if it turns out that you've chosen them for the wrong reasons.

I'm going to tell you something about alpha males that you might not already know – but if you're going to be one, it's something you'll need to embrace. Alpha males have enough respect for themselves and their own opinions and choices that, most of the time, they will go with their own ideas rather than bow to the will of the crowd.

If common wisdom tells you that you ought to be in bed by 10 o'clock but you know full well that you're at your most creative or motivated after midnight, you need to be strong enough in yourself to go with what YOU know is right for you.

If your guidance counselor told you that you ought to go into construction, but your heart is telling you that you want to be a vet or a chef or a doctor, or even a rock star, then you need to respect your own thoughts on the matter and choose to follow what YOU think is best career for you.

If your team wants you to play lineman when you know you'd be perfect as quarterback, it's up to YOU to not just tell them that they're wrong, but prove that what you're saying is really the case.

You see what I'm getting at here? It doesn't matter what other people are saying, you are an independent man with his own thoughts, attitudes and opinions and, just because someone else doesn't agree with them, that doesn't make them wrong.

It's time to start thinking and acting that way. Let's say you find yourself in a discussion about politics and your sparring partner leans a different way to you. It's not your job to sit and listen to him and agree with what he's saying, and I doubt you even think it is right now. But, on the other hand, taking your own stand does not mean simply shouting the other person down. It means hearing what they say and searching your own repertoire of knowledge and experience to decipher it, then making up your mind based on everything you now know. It means considered, thoughtful responses to the opinions of others.

In a nutshell, that's what being an alpha male is all about. I'm not telling you to stop listening to other people, because that's one of the best and most useful ways to gather new information, and information is how you grow.

I'm telling you that it's your responsibility to process that data and to come to your own conclusions at the end. And I'm also telling you that you need to stop being afraid of those conclusions, because an alpha male has the self respect, and the respect for other people, to compare his own beliefs against the new information he's been given, and come to his own judgment by doing so.

This is also a major step towards becoming a natural leader. Think about the best leaders you've encountered during your life and you'll see that they all have one thing in common. They're confident enough in themselves to welcome input from everyone around them; strong minded enough to surround themselves with people of equal strength and knowledge; and respectful enough of themselves and their followers to digest that information and use it to come to the best conclusion possible.

As an alpha male, your ultimate goal is to be the kind of person people look to when they need leadership. You want them to trust you to be able to come to the right conclusions and not simply do what you're being told to do. It might seem terrifying at first, especially if you're used to bowing down to other people's wishes, but you'll find out fast that it's a supremely satisfying feeling.

* * * * *

Before we continue, I have a small favor to ask:

Could you please take a minute of your time to write an
honest review of the book?

Your reviews are what keeps me going. I read every single
one of them, and would be **extremely thankful** if you
choose to share your thoughts with me.

* * * * *

Take Control of Every Situation

I'm going to start by giving you three example scenarios. I want you to read each one, then spend a couple of minutes applying them to a similar but real situation from your own past. It doesn't matter if you haven't found yourself in the exact same situation, you just need to apply it as closely as you're able to to your own life.

I want you to think about the role you took in that real life situation – while it was unfolding, what exactly were you doing?

1) Your boss calls a meeting to announce a new project for the company. It's a big one and a departure from what everyone has done before. He's going to need to put a team together and every person on that team is going to need to contribute to the success of the project in some way.

2) Your friends decide it's high time you all went on a trip together, somewhere exotic or with adventure sports and women aplenty. First, you're going to need to decide where everyone wants to go. Then, someone is going to need to take charge of arranging the dates, flights, hotels, itinerary and

other arrangements.

3)   Your best friend is about to get married and is
     putting together the wedding party. His biggest
     priority is that he wants a completely awesome
     bachelor party, complete with all the trimmings,
     and people who will take the load off when it
     comes to the dull details of arranging the rest of the
     wedding.

You've read the scenarios and thought about what you
were doing in a similar real life situation. Write it down –
go on, be a man. That way I'll know you weren't lying.

Here's what an alpha male would do in those scenarios. I
wonder how close you came...

1)   The alpha male wouldn't hesitate to step forward
     and offer to take charge of the project, right there in
     front of everyone. He would immediately start
     mentally planning the structure of the team,
     thinking about everyone's strengths and
     weaknesses and who would work well together.
     He already knows all these things, because he's a
     social animal who pays genuine attention to the
     people around him. He's also not afraid of the
     stress levels of a brand new project, because
     opportunities like this are what drive him. He's not

worried that the team will fail, because if they do
he can just make the right changes and try again.
And he's not concerned about handling the conflict,
because he's unflappable and will not be affected
by the adversity.

2) An alpha male will know straight away what kind
of vacation will suit his group of friends – and if he
can't immediately think of a destination that will
suit everyone equally, he'll turn his mind to finding
ways to make up the difference. He won't feel it
necessary to handle all the arrangements, but he'll
oversee them and it's to him that the volunteers
will report what they've been doing – naturally,
and without questioning why he's taken the lead. If
people argue about what's being planned, he'll
defuse the situation affably and quickly. And he'll
be the one who everyone follows around when
they get to their vacation spot, too.

3) Obviously, without any question at all, an alpha
would be the perfect best man. Calm and collected
enough to handle the sheer stress levels of a
wedding and naturally able to take charge and
delegate to others, he's also got the self confidence
to know that this isn't his day – it isn't his moment
to shine. Without even the need to consider it, he'll

do everything necessary to make his friend's day a success, turning the spotlight that so often shines on him onto his friend, instead. He'll support his friend with an unwavering sense of confidence that everything's going to be a success, letting him lean when he needs to do, and he'll do all of this completely without effort, because that's just the type of guy he is.

Did you react to these situations in the past like an alpha male would? Were any of your reactions on the list? Or were you the second in command, the naysayer or the follower? I'm willing to bet you ticked off a couple of the alpha male's reactions. You're reading this book, which means you have a natural inclination towards the alpha, which means you'll doubtless have fulfilled at least a couple of his roles sometime in your past.

But I doubt you reacted exactly how an alpha male would, or you wouldn't need to be following this guide. So it's time to change all that – from now on, you'll need to step up and take charge of every situation you find yourself in. And if it's hard at first, you'll need to keep trying until it becomes second nature.

Why is it that an alpha male is always in charge, no matter what the scenario is and whether he actually has any functional experience of handling it? Because he's the one who knows how to handle things – he knows how to be a leader.

The alpha male has a plan when it comes to taking charge, and you'll need to devise your own. And while that does take some experience, you can think about it beforehand and come up with ideas for how you would arrange your teams, deal with conflict, sort out problems and divide the work.

Here's how: put yourself in your boss's shoes and walk through his day. Decide how you would handle each of the things he has to handle – would you do it the same way, or would you do it differently? Why? And why do you think your way is better?

And mark my words, it IS ok to think your way is better. In fact, it's one of the keys to your success. An alpha male doesn't just follow another man's way of doing things. He has his own ways and methods, and he has confidence that they are the best ways.

Here's a little secret: that alpha male who always seems to get the best projects and everyone follows about on nights out with the boys? He doesn't know nearly as much about what he's doing as it seems. What he does know is how to portray himself as a natural leader, and you can do exactly the same. But, to do it, you'll need to work on a few of your personality traits, and that's not going to be as easy as you think.

- Keep your cool in every situation, no matter how much hurt, anger and negativity is boiling under the surface.

- When faced with a new challenge you know nothing about, don't turn it down. Remember that your role as alpha male is to take charge of the project, not necessarily to be the person with the knowledge and experience to carry it through.

- Nurture friendships with as many people as you can, from as many walks of life, as many different departments in your company, as many clubs and groups and societies and with as many skills as you can. When you're faced with a challenge, you want to be able to call on these people to help you complete it.

- Learn how to listen to other people and really hear what they're saying. An alpha male is a team leader – he's the guy in charge, the one who listens to problems and issues and directs people towards solutions. Most of the time, that's as easy as helping someone choose between option A, B and C.

- Think in terms of gathering information, on a constant basis and from as many sources as you can. When you're faced with problems from here on out, whether you're in a leadership position or not, don't settle for just asking one person or looking it up on one website. Start thinking about finding a variety of resources and delving deeper to answer every question. Why do alpha males do that? Because they can be trusted to make informed decisions based on as many sources of information as possible and with all possibilities given equal thought.

What you may have noticed from these traits is that an alpha male might be your mailman, he might be the President of the United States or a bartender. He could be a teacher at your local school, the leader of your local soccer team or the CEO of a Forbes 100 company. It doesn't matter what he does or where he does it, it matters how he does it. The context is irrelevant: it's all about consistently coping with situations by taking the lead, and taking it well.

If you can develop the skills to bring people together and coax them in the right direction, and show them that you can be trusted to make decisions on their behalf? Well, if you can do that, the battle to become an alpha male is halfway won.

- Learn to delegate. An alpha male achieves a hell of a lot in a single day, but he also knows how to get other people working alongside him towards the right goals. If you've never had people to delegate to before, you'll find pretty quickly that, as you adopt the alpha male persona, people start expecting you to take control and are ready and willing to be delegated to. But before you can do that, you'll need to let go of the inclination to take on every little task yourself. That can be hard, especially if you're a perfectionist, because you run the constant risk that tasks won't get done right, on time or in the way you would have done them. But if you don't learn to do it, you won't get people into the groove of working how you want to work, and things won't ever improve.

- Always stay calm. If you're hot headed, you already know that adversity can cause your head to explode with rage in the space of a moment. Someone scratches your brand new motorcycle, you get hit with an unfair bill, the train is late again. These little niggles get to the best of us, and reacting with rage is something we all want to do. But an alpha male never lets these things get the

best of him. So next time someone flips your
triggers and makes you want to rage quit the day,
take the deepest breath you can muster. Let go of
the rage, even if it takes you an hour of just
standing there, inert and pointless as a lamp post.
And once you have, you can turn your attention to
reacting in an effective and constructive manner.
Call the responsible party, find a new route to get
home – whatever it takes to fix the problem. As you
keep working on this, the time it takes for your
rage to subside will lessen until you are able to let
go immediately, deal with the problem and move
on. That's what an alpha male does – and that's
why everyone looks to him straight away in the
event of an emergency.

- **Control your reaction, not the situation.** If you're
  finding it hard to understand the difference
  between an alpha male's attitude and your own,
  perhaps this exercise might help. Next time you get
  hit with an unexpected problem, repeat this mantra
  to yourself: I cannot change the fact that this is
  happening, but I CAN control what I do about it.
  An alpha male always controls his own emotions in
  a bad situation, never loses his cool and always
  chooses logic over emotion. You'll need to learn to
  let go of your impotent rage, but you're also going

to need to work on understanding that the situation
might be out of control, but your reaction to it most
certainly isn't – and it's your reaction that counts,
because that's what people will see and that's what
will make them think of you as a leader.

Above All Else, Be Yourself

So far, everything that I've told you in this book has involved improving yourself, changing yourself and generally not being the same person you were a few days ago, when you handed over your pennies to buy this guide in the hopes it would change your life. What I'm going to tell you now is a little bit different to all that. Think of this as a pause before the big push at the end: we've ramped up, got you going in the right direction, booted you up the ass when you decided it was all too hard and turned your eyes towards the prize.

Now it's time for a look inward. Because, if there's one thing I know about the process of becoming an alpha male, it's that it's filled with stumbling blocks and traps that can very easily get in your way. I touched on this at the start, but you need a reminder, lest you forget why it is that you're doing this.

You decided to become an alpha male because you felt that you had it in you. You weren't completely happy with who and what you were, but you also didn't hate that person completely. Remember me telling you that being an alpha male is not about putting on a front and pretending to be something you aren't? At this point, you might be wondering if that was me blowing smoke up your butt. I'm pushing you to get confident, change how you act, even change how you think. Doesn't that count as putting on a front?

No, because I want you to mean it. I want you to make these changes gradually and, over time, come to accept them not as the actions of a different person, but the ultimate version of yourself.

I want you to become what all the hipsters and hippies out there would describe as "the very best version of yourself". Even if that phrase makes you gag, and I'll tell you right now it does me, just think about it for a second. You're not an alpha male, but you're an ok guy – it's just that you're not pushing your potential. You're not an alpha male, but you have the potential to be, you have positive traits and you're likeable – it's just that you haven't pushed any of these things to see how far you can go.

So if you've been reading this guide so far and feeling sorry for yourself because half the things I'm telling you to do aren't things you think are possible for you, it's time to step back and reassess. That's just not true, and when you're not feeling nervous, overwhelmed or plain lazy, you know it.

Not the best ball player in the world? What does that matter in the grand scheme of things? I'm not telling you that, to become an alpha male, you'll have to outplay the Denver Broncos. I'm telling you that you need to embrace your passion for the game and give it every last little bit that you've got.

Not the best at organization? Not the most attractive dude in the class? Not brilliant at talking to women? None of these things matter. What matters is that you have a genuine love for everything you do, and that it shows. It matters that you give it all you've got, and that it shows. Understand what I'm saying? It's all about you finding out who and what you love and doing everything in your power to make those things part of your life.

Alpha males don't get to that point because they're already the best at what they try. They take their place in their own eyes, and in the eyes of everyone around them, because they are attacking every challenge with confidence and never giving up.

So when I tell you that I want you to be yourself, I mean that I want you to look again at your talents, skills, character and so on, recognize that a lot of it is already something to be proud of – and then push every single one of them until you're the proudest you can possibly be.

Get What You Want – Whatever It Is

So here we are, nearing the end of your crash course in becoming an alpha male. Feeling better about yourself yet? Maybe a little bit, right? But not completely, because you haven't started seeing many returns for your efforts.

So let's start reaping a few, shall we? Let's turn everything we've learned towards the things you've been pining for – the things that made you want to do this in the first place.

Let me list them for you, because I'm pretty sure you know what they are: you want a rockin' body, the girl of your dreams, the career everyone envies and friends who envy your lifestyle.

So let's finish this by looking at those things one by one, and working out how you're going to get them. As you're about to find out, everything we've been doing up until this point has been geared towards helping your dreams come true.

Confidence, when it comes to women, is key. The reason I pushed you so hard to work on your confidence is that it's like an aphrodisiac to a woman: she can sense it, and she wants it. As an alpha male, women will be chasing you, not the other way around. And they'll be doing that because they sense that you're a man worth claiming, because you have goals and aspirations and you're clearly going somewhere with your life. Once you're done working on your confidence, the hard part is over.

So what else do you need to do?

- First up, find your protective instinct – the one that makes you want to run to a loved one's rescue when they're in trouble. An alpha male always protects his friends and his family, and a woman finds that irresistible.

- Next, quit being scared of rejection. So you decide to talk to a pretty girl and she snubs you before you can ask her for her name. So what? She's not the only fish in the sea, and you're not going to find out if she's interested until you try asking her. An alpha male wouldn't let it stop him – he wouldn't care. An alpha male takes risks without a second thought, knowing that's the only way he can really push his boundaries. Stay in your comfort zone and you'll never meet any women at all, let alone the woman of your dreams. Step outside it and she'll notice – and she'll want you even more.

- Now, stop being such a desperate dick. The more you convince yourself you need a woman in your life to be happy, the less attractive you become. A woman wants a man who knows what he wants and isn't afraid to go out and get it, not one who hangs back and stares like a latchkey kid as his friends chat her up. Women like a challenge as much as men do, and a desperate man is not a challenge. He's someone she can fall back on if her other options don't pan out – do you really want to be her third choice?

- Finally, start giving those women you're interested in the respect that they deserve. The second you start thinking of them as commodities – something you should have or need to own – you're doomed. A true alpha male wants a partner who complements him completely. He wants a woman, or a man, who has her own goals, hopes and dreams. And to get a woman like that, you need to respect her and show her that you don't need to dominate or possess her. You are happy to let her be her own person and it doesn't worry you if that means having a more successful career or attracting the attention of other men. That, after all, is what you'll love about her in the first place. And because she knows that, she will love you more than you can even imagine.

You've always wanted killer abs and the kind of butt that women's eyes follow down the street. Haven't we all? But have you done anything about it, yet? This aspect of your journey is both about becoming an alpha male and reaping the rewards of doing so. If you want to be a true alpha, it's something you can't avoid. But because you ARE becoming a true alpha, it's something you now have the willpower, confidence and determination to accomplish.

Your body is a reflection of the inner you – it shows people what you are like on the inside and what your priorities are. And being as how two of the most important traits you want people to know about you are that you take pride in yourself and that you have strength of character, your body will show people that you value yourself, and that you are worth valuing.

- Pay attention to your grooming. From here on out, I don't want to see you leave the house with your hair mussed and before you've taken a shower, and definitely not in yesterday's clothes. I'm not suggesting you start spending longer in the bathroom than your sister or girlfriend, but I do want you to look in the mirror every time you leave the house and ask yourself: If I saw this man, would I respect him?

- Get yourself into a routine. You're going to need to start exercising, be it with weights, at the gym or via your favorite sport. The only way you can do that is to set yourself targets and goals and get yourself into the habit of working out. If you're tired, tough luck. If you'd rather go out on the tiles, tough luck. If you've got too much other stuff to do, tough luck. Making working out your priority, because it's the only way you're going to improve the way you look and get yourself in shape.

- Start thinking about this as just another part of your day. Those guys you see who constantly preen and wear tight tops so you can see their pecs, and won't talk about anything but protein powder and the new machine they have at the gym? That's not an alpha male, that's not you. You need to think of it as a change you're making for life, and when you start to see the results you need to take joy and pride in them and use them to fuel tomorrow's efforts.

- Get some help figuring out what you need to do to get your ideal body. Hire a trainer for a while and get them to show you how to lose the extra pounds or gain some muscle on your scrawny arms. They can tell you what it's possible to improve, and they can show you how to do it. The rest? That's up to you.

An alpha male is a natural leader, and that's why he always wins jobs and gets promotions, climbing to the top of his field faster than anyone else. He's also driven and dedicated, as we've already covered.

But maybe you don't want to be a CEO and you don't want to trade shares on Wall Street. Maybe you want to be a writer or a fisherman, make furniture or play professional sports.

With being an alpha male, you'll find that authority comes naturally. It's all about being confident in yourself and inspiring confidence in others, and it's about treating people with genuine interest and respect such that they feel valued and appreciated and want to follow you.

It's the same story as it was back in medieval battles – men followed their knights, dukes and kings into hell and fought and died for them simply because they believed so strongly in that leader. Think those dudes were anything but alpha males? Of course not.

If you want to embrace that side effect of becoming an alpha male, more power to you. Make sure that you understand that great power brings great responsibility and that you'll need to take a genuine care for the people you are leading and always, always, be as mindful of their own needs and hopes as your own.

If you don't, you can still make use of your newfound leadership abilities. You can use your charm and power to win people round to your way of thinking through reasoned, thoughtful discussions and a willingness to listen. But, in this case, you can use it to win clients, opportunities or customers. You can use your leadership abilities to ramp up what you're doing, build a team to help you achieve your goals. Your determination and drive will be infectious – use it to convince other people to help you, invest in you or otherwise join your cause. Your streamlined focus will help you set goals for yourself and then meet them.

Being an alpha male doesn't mean you have to work in the banking industry. It doesn't mean you have to climb to the lofty ranks of the CEOs and COOs and C-whatever elses. It means you need to push the bounds of whatever career you want to follow – and that you need to choose the career based on your deepest and most beloved passions.

Get the Lifestyle

There's one secret, and just one secret, to getting the lifestyle you want: you have to take it. We talked before about blazing your own path and not being afraid to take chances and make decisions that other people haven't necessarily approved of. The same goes for getting the lifestyle you want: nobody is going to give it to you, so it's up to you to decide what it is and then take it.

- Stop fearing the idea of taking a risk. There's only one way to banish fear, and that's to power through it. If the lifestyle you want means changing a lot about what you currently have, don't be surprised if you come up against a brick wall of fear at some point along the way. Expect to, and make up your mind right now to power through that wall. Alpha males don't let a little thing like fear stand in their way.

- Ignore anyone who is trying to tell you that you're wrong, or not good enough, or that something isn't possible. People always talk from their own perspectives and can't put themselves in your shoes. They think you can't work four days a week and play for three because their own finances, career choices of family life wouldn't allow it. That doesn't mean you can't. They think you're wrong to drop a promising career to become an artist or an architect or, hell, a deep sea diver. That's because they wouldn't have the guts to do it themselves, but it doesn't mean you can't. They tell you that you're not good enough because they're jealous, or because it makes them feel better about their own failures. Ignore them – but learn to tell the difference between naysayers and people who give constructive advice. If someone is offering you useful information and opinions, an alpha male will always add that to his arsenal.

- Take stock of what you've got and what you want. Don't bother being realistic – that comes later. Dream big and tell yourself you want to be draped in Playboy models on your own private yacht in the Seychelles. Now work out how you're going to get there – remember, an alpha male is all about the planning. He knows what he wants and he works out how to get it. No matter how big or small your dream, it's up to you to clear the path to it.

- Keep working on your confidence. The reason alpha males get what they want is that they have the confidence to know they deserve it and can have it as long as they earn it. The more confident you are, the better your chances of reaching those dreams and getting your ideal lifestyle.

In your life so far, you'll have met plenty of alpha males. I want you to list as many of them as you can remember. Next to their names, I want you to note the personality traits that you most admired in those men, and why.

After a while, you'll come to a realization: what you admire in most of them will be the same characteristics. It might be their winning charm, their affable good nature or their drive and determination. What you'll find is that there are traits linking all the men you most admire – and these are the traits you secretly want for yourself.

So now, it's time to dig deep within yourself and get them. Pick just one of those men, one that you absolutely respect and admire and would like to become. Make that choice the person that embodies all the traits you don't feel confident about yet in yourself, but you wish you did. Next time you find yourself in a situation that you know you haven't handled in the past as an alpha male would, ask yourself what that man would do in your place.

This might seem like just pretending to be someone else, but it's not wish fulfillment and you're not going to win an Oscar. You're channeling what you already know through a single person who embodies the traits you want to nurture. That's a complicated way of saying that you already have these traits, you recognize them in this person you're so in awe of and the easiest way to access those traits is to look through that man's eyes at your behavior. It's a little trick that will help you see yourself objectively and start to work on the personality you wish you'd always had. Trust me, it works.

Stop Reading, Start Doing

Are you wiping off what I'm spitting yet? Are you picking up what I'm putting down? Have you caught my drift?

Becoming an alpha male is not a pipe dream and it's not something that only certain guys can achieve. Whoever and wherever you are, you can do this. You just have one final step to take.

Now you know what to do and what you'll need to achieve to transform yourself into an alpha male, all that remains is to get out there and do it. Set your goals, make your plans, find your hero and change your thinking.

Start going to the gym, start taking some risks, stop letting your fears get in the way of what you want. I've told you how you can get everything you ever dreamed of. It's up to you now to go out there and get it.

You have the opportunity, the tools and the ability to change your life forever, just by following the advice I've given you. As long as you stick to it and never let yourself lapse back into the thinking that held you back until now, you can transform yourself into an alpha male.

You can change things – by changing yourself. You are the only thing standing between yourself and the women, wine and song you've been pining for all along.

Would an alpha male let that stand? Would he sit there and wait for things to change? Would he ignore opportunity and convince himself it couldn't be done?

Of course he wouldn't. So what are you waiting for?

Special Thanks

I would like to give special thanks to all the readers from around the globe who chose to share their kind and encouraging words with me.

Knowing even just one person found this book helpful means the world to me.

If you've benefited from this book at all, I would be honored to have you share your thoughts on it, so that others would get something valuable out of this book too.

Your reviews are the fuel for my writing soul, and I'd be **<u>forever grateful</u>** to see *your* review, too.

Thank you all!

9 789659 297627